NATURALLY WILD MUSICIANS

THE WONDROUS WORLD OF ANIMAL SONG

Peter Christie

annick press
toronto + new york + vancouver

For P, singer of chansons

Text © 2007 Peter Christie

Annick Press Ltd.

We acknowledge the support of the Canada Council for the Arts, the Ontario Arts Council, the Government of Canada through the Book Publishing Industry Development Program (BPIDP), and the Ontario Book Publishing Tax Credit (OBPTC) for our publishing activities.

Edited by Elizabeth McLean
Cover and interior design by Li Eng-Lodge, Electra Design Group
Photo research by Antonia Banyard

Cataloguing in Publication

Christie, Peter, 1962–
 Naturally wild musicians : the wondrous world of animal song / by Peter Christie.

Includes bibliographical references and index.
ISBN-13: 978-1-55451-098-6 (bound)
ISBN-10: 1-55451-098-8 (bound)
ISBN-13: 978-1-55451-097-9 (pbk)
ISBN-10: 1-55451-097-X (pbk.)

 1. Sound production by animals—Juvenile literature. 2. Animal sounds—Juvenile literature. I. Title.

QL765.C47 2007   j591.59'4   C2007-900700-7

Printed and bound in China

Published in the U.S.A. by
Annick Press (U.S.) Ltd.

Distributed in Canada by
Firefly Books Ltd.
66 Leek Crescent
Richmond Hill, ON
L4B 1H1

Distributed in the U.S.A. by
Firefly Books (U.S.) Inc.
P.O. Box 1338
Ellicott Station
Buffalo, NY 14205

Visit our website at **www.annickpress.com**

Contents

Love Songs & Battle Hymns

After his pet starling died, Mozart composed music that many believe mimics the bird's style.

When his friend died in 1789, the Austrian musician arranged a grand funeral. Mourners in veils marched slowly to the burial site. The crowd sang hymns, and the musician read a poem written for the occasion.

The Austrian was Wolfgang Amadeus Mozart, one of the greatest composers in history. He had lost his adored roommate—and source of musical inspiration for the past three years. Standing over the new grave, Mozart bid goodbye to his companion, a European starling.

Chir-r-rp! Katydids make music by scraping the sharp edge of one front wing along a file-like ridge on the other.

Mozart loved his starling because it sang beautifully. It inspired the musician's genius, just as the melodies of birds and other creatures have always moved people. Other composers owe a debt to nature's music too, and so do centuries of poets.

Although song may evoke deep human feeling, it has a different purpose in the world of animals. The music-makers are usually males, performing during the breeding season. Their tunes let females know where to find a good mate, or tell other males to stay away. They're the creature equivalent of love songs and battle hymns, often rolled into one tune.

Some scientists disagree about what is or isn't animal song. But songs are generally considered different from animal calls. Calls are used throughout the year and are usually not related to mating. Songs are often performed during particular weeks or months and at specific times of day. American toads, for instance, sing through

the night in early spring. American robins warble at sunrise and sunset well into the summer.

Animal songs are specifically for courtship and defending a breeding territory. A musical performance can make or break the singer's chance of finding a mate and having young.

Some animals, such as Mozart's starling, sing complex songs with many notes and phrases. Other creatures, such as insects, frogs, and even some fish, produce far simpler sounds.

Not every animal sings its song; some play their tunes. Crickets and

American robins and other songbirds sing at dawn or dusk when there's usually less wind to muffle the sound.

katydids fiddle their music, rubbing one wing against the other. Some catfish grasp the whiskers of a female with one fin and play a short song to her with the other. Club-winged manakins are birds, but prefer to produce a loud *tick-tick-ting* song by strumming their wings with special feather tips.

Scientists are learning just how important song is to the animal kingdom. They are also discovering that music is used by a surprising variety of creatures.

Birds are the best-known singers, but even male gray mouse lemurs, a tiny relative of monkeys, trill to attract mates.

chapter 1

Mating
Chords of Courtship

Rrrruuuummmm

The droning music of plainfir midshipman fish sounds like an underwater beehive.

ouseboats anchored along the California coast rise and fall on the summer swells. The lights of San Francisco can be seen in the distance, but out here it's dark and peaceful.

Rrrrrrrrrummmmmmmm … Huh? What could that be?

Rrrrrrrrummmmmmmm … The noise—part growl and part drone—grows louder. It sounds like a flotilla of motorboats or an enormous hive of bees, or even the deep chanting of monks. In summers past, some people have blamed the military and secret testing offshore.

How could the sleepless houseboaters guess the truth? The noisemakers are actually fish—plainfin midshipman fish— and they're singing to attract females.

Every spring, these fish migrate from the depths of the Pacific Ocean to shallower waters along the coast where they mate. Males dig a nest in the sand and hum their loud, monotonous tune by vibrating their swim bladder—an internal air sac that helps fish to swim upward or to dive by adjusting their buoyancy. Singers can keep up the noise for as long as 15 minutes.

A female that likes what she hears will enter a singer's lair, lay all her eggs, and promptly swim away. The male will guard the eggs until they hatch and grow. And he will continue to sing, hoping to attract more egg-laying females.

The song is loud. In fact, it's loud enough to deafen the singers themselves. But scientists have discovered that the same area of their fishy brain that controls sound production also controls hearing. When the fish start their bladders humming, they reduce the sensitivity of their ears at exactly the same time.

Rrrruuuuuum

Buzzz

Attracting a mate is one of the main purposes of animal song. Many songs work like advertising jingles: they help "sell" singing males to the females that hear them. Females listen for clues that can tell them who's hot and who's not when selecting a mate.

Musical advertising works well because it can be heard from far away, or even through dense or leafy terrain that would hide visual displays or fancy good looks. This suits cicadas just fine. Cicadas are stocky, bug-eyed insects and not likely to win any beauty contests judged by humans. But they can sure sing.

Cicadas make their buzzy music from trees. Like many singing insects, cicadas

Adult cicadas have only a few weeks to live—and sing—after spending up to 17 years as larvae underground.

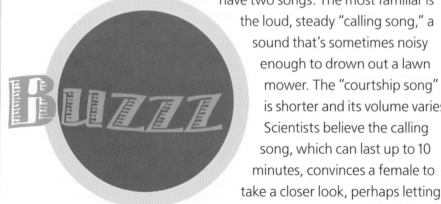

have two songs. The most familiar is the loud, steady "calling song," a sound that's sometimes noisy enough to drown out a lawn mower. The "courtship song" is shorter and its volume varies. Scientists believe the calling song, which can last up to 10 minutes, convinces a female to take a closer look, perhaps letting her know that the singer belongs to her species.

The courtship song is used when the singer and an interested female are close to each other. Courtship songs are sometimes accompanied by a kind of wing-flick dance to which the female responds with wing flicks of her own. The precise roles of the courtship song or the wing-flick duet aren't well understood, but they're clearly important to successful mating.

Red deer stags bellow across forests and fields to attract females to join their herd.

In the fall, male European red deer bellow through the forest in a series of low roars. For listening females, the tempo of the serenade seems to matter most.

Red deer males are called stags, and they usually travel with a herd of up to 20 females, called hinds. Hinds leave or join the herd as they please. Stags that roar at a fast rate attract more females that stick around than stags that roar more slowly. Roaring, like shouting, is difficult to do repeatedly. The hinds may prefer rapid roaring because it shows that the stag has strength and stamina to defend the herd from other male deer.

A Hermann's tortoise is an unlikely crooner, but his song will help convince a female that he's Mr. Right.

The Tuneful Tortoise

In the dry hills above the Mediterranean Sea, a small black-and-yellow Hermann's tortoise lumbers through his long life the way most tortoises do—in plodding, ponderous silence.

Noiselessly, he searches for a female. Without a sound, he spies one nearby. Quietly, he pursues her through grass and brush until at last she stops. Finally, when he climbs onto her back in an attempt to mate, the male tortoise does something few reptiles ever do: he breaks into song.

Scientists believe the sound—a shrill whimpering—helps convince females to breed. Although a male may chase and mount a female, her cooperation is needed to mate successfully. Females prefer high-pitched, rapid singing that might mean a singer is strong and healthy.

Female great reed warblers prefer males that sing the greatest number of song types.

chapter 2

Rivals

Singing Duels & Territorial Tunes

The tiny chickadee fights his battles with songs, not swords.

I n a dense maple forest in southern Canada, two adversaries prepare to duel. The battleground is a patch of woods no bigger than a soccer field. Chins high and chests out, the contestants face each other.

A challenge is issued. In the language of black-capped chickadees it sounds like *Chickadee-dee-dee.* The other bird answers instantly: *"Fee bee-ee,"* he sings in two clear notes.

"Fee bee-ee," sings his adversary in slightly higher notes.

The first singer transposes his song to exactly match the musical pitch of his foe: *"Fee bee-ee."*

"Fee …"

"Fee bee-ee." This time, the first singer overlaps the song of his adversary. The contest is all but over. Matching the notes is like striking a rival's sword in fencing. Matching the notes and overlapping the song is like striking swords and following through with a thrust.

Many animals use song to defend territories during the breeding season. Songs can often be heard from one end of a creature's turf to the other. Just as a singer's performance can tell a female whether a male would make a good mate, it can also signal to other males whether a singer is a weakling worth challenging or a hotshot that would hold his own in a fight.

For chickadees, song duels can determine which contestant is top bird without a dangerous physical battle.

chickadee-dee dee

fee bee-ee

The chorus of the male coqui frogs is intended for other coqui frogs, but in Hawaii it has hotel owners and island residents hopping mad. Coqui frogs are small tree frogs, and they have an extraordinary voice for such a little animal. The frog's two-note *ko-kee* can reach noise levels close to that of a chainsaw.

Researchers believe the first and loudest part of the song is aimed at other males. Males answer the *ko* note of other males. The volume of replies helps them to keep their distance and avoid a fight.

Talk about noisy visitors! The small coqui frog brought its big voice to Hawaii, but not everyone appreciates the sound.

Ko-kee

Ko-kee

Ko-kee

The frogs are native to Puerto Rico, but they have invaded three of Hawaii's islands and their numbers have soared in less than a decade. Hawaiians are not used to frog songs, much less extremely loud ones—there are no amphibians native to the islands. They are worried that the din will keep tourists away. Researchers are seeking ways to control these noisy aliens, which can reach densities of 20,000 frogs in an area smaller than most city blocks in their homeland forests of Puerto Rico.

The loud tok-kay of male tokay geckos may warn other males away, while attracting females.

Sometimes animals use many different songs to defend their territories. Song sparrows, for instance, are common North American birds that sing a number of complicated tunes.

Why some creatures need a variety of songs is not well understood. But scientists believe variety might help these birds resolve disputes. Song sparrows living next to one another often share several of the same songs. They also sing other songs that are not shared. When one bird wants to sound threatening, he'll sing one of the tunes he shares with his neighbor. If he's really upset, he'll precisely match his neighbor's melody.

To avoid a physical fight, a song sparrow can switch to a tune that is not shared by his neighbor. Knowing many songs gives them a way to make peace.

Song sparrows know a range of songs, and use them to pick a fight or to help avoid one.

Make song, not war. Atlantic walrus males can avoid deadly fights by giving long musical performances.

TAP
KNOCK
RING

Polar Pavarotti

High in the Canadian arctic, a herd of Atlantic walruses huddles on an ice floe. They watch the frigid water as the great polar Pavarotti—an enormous male walrus—performs his aria. He dives and begins a series of knock-like sounds and bell-like ringing from deep in his throat. Singing with his mouth closed, he can be heard through the ice. *Tap, knock, ring.*

Each rhythmic song can last up to seven minutes. A single performance of many singing dives by one of these great northern creatures can last up to 65 hours. Scientists believe the music warns other walruses to stay away from the singing male's harem of females. Since territorial tusk fights between males are bloody and sometimes deadly, it pays to be tuneful.

chapter 3

Recognition

Songs of the Guess Who

The whirring song of a male American toad tells females if the singer is a family membe[r]

Male American toads float in the pond's duckweed and fill the late April night with song. They have returned to the wetlands of their birth to breed. Their chorus is shrill and steady, and individual songs weave together into a monumental knot of sound.

From this, females hope to follow one musical strand to just the right male. Low voices belong to big males. Faster, longer songs belong to strong, healthy singers. Low, long, and fast make for an attractive tune. But the females are listening for something else as well.

Toads that breed in their home ponds are likely to meet brothers and sisters there. For most animals, mating with siblings or other close kin is a bad idea. It often leads to young that don't survive or have serious genetic problems.

Researchers have found that toad songs tell females whether a singer is a close relative. Females prefer tunes sung by unrelated toads.

Animal songs let others know who is singing. This is important to females, and can signal whether a singer is the same species, or even a relative. It's also important to males keeping track of neighbors.

A male hooded warbler, for example, can identify neighbors by melody. He keeps track of them, and can detect the songs of an intruder.

In a forest full of warblers, remembering the song signatures of five or six neighbors is an impressive feat for a bird brain. More impressive still, hooded warblers remember their neighbors' songs from year to year, despite eight months apart each winter when they fly south.

Only humans had previously been shown to remember individuals over such a long period. But it serves the warblers well. They return to almost the same territory each breeding season and are spared having to relearn their neighbors' music.

ruit flies may seem insignificant, but they're sophisticated musicians. Male fruit flies perform by vibrating their wings, and their song is an important part of courtship.

In northern Scandinavia, four different fruit fly species breed at almost the same time. The flies gather on rotting plants and fruit, and a courtship free-for-all takes place. Males of one species often woo females of another.

Song sorts it out. When a female responds to his courting, a male will sing. It's the make-or-break moment for many fruit fly romances. Males sing songs typical of their species. If the music doesn't jive with that of the female's species, she loses interest.

He's singing my song. Female fruit flies can tell by the tune if a male fruit fly is the same species.

Bicolor damselfish keep track of sneaky neighbors by listening for their characteristic song.

chirp

chirp

Male leopard seals perform loud, underwater trills—distinctive enough to identify the singer.

Familiar Songs that Sound Fishy

If male bicolor damselfish had a favorite sign, it would be "No Trespassing." This coral reef fish is no bigger than a cell phone, but it fiercely protects its turf from other fish and, in particular, other damselfish. Damselfish territories usually contain prized coral nesting sites and provide a stage for courtship performances.

Bicolor damselfish are among a number of fishes that sing. Males perform their *chirp* song while swimming up a short distance and diving quickly down to attract mates. Researchers have found that male bicolor damselfish not only listen to the songs of neighbors, but can identify who is singing, possibly by their musical pitch. It's a useful skill for keeping track of neighbors that may sneak across a boundary to claim the territory as their own.

chapter 4

Broadcasting Mud Megaphone & Tree-hole Opera

Practice makes perfect. Borneo tree-hole frog tries to find the right note to fit his woody music studio.

As evening closes on a damp Florida field, an ingenious maker of musical instruments is at work. A male southern mole cricket positions himself near the funnel-shaped entrance to his burrow and calls. *Chirp.* He tests the sound and adjusts the burrow until his homemade bugle is just right.

In the same way a trumpet's shape improves its sound, the burrow is fine-tuned to perfectly suit the cricket's musical pitch, or tone. Its burrow can amplify the insect's song enough to be heard up to six football fields away, to attract females flying overhead.

A good horn not only helps male crickets to be heard, but also increases their appeal. Female mole crickets prefer loud songs. Researchers have found that male crickets increase the volume even more by digging in wet soil. The damp ground prevents sound from escaping through tiny spaces in the sand, making the mud megaphone louder.

Songs that carry a long way are important to musical creatures. They need to be heard by their intended audience. Many animals sing tunes suited to broadcast well in the places they live. Others get broadcasting help from features in their environment.

On the island of Borneo, male tree-hole frogs sing from tree-hole "opera houses." Each fist-sized hole is partly filled with rainwater so it doubles as a breeding pool. A male sings his chorus of rich *peeps* from the hole, trying to entice females to lay eggs there.

The cavities help amplify the frog's song, but only if he's singing the right note. Just as a particular pitch is tuned to the size and shape of an organ pipe, only a small set of sounds perfectly fits the size and shape of a tree hole. The frogs peep, listen, and then peep again, experimenting until they hit just the right pitch to pump up the volume.

Water carries the wistful tun of humpback whales across huge distance

The songs of humpback whales travel far. In fact, they have been recorded at distances equal to a two-hour car journey. The whales' music of haunting whistles and squeals is among the most spectacular in the animal world. Their long arias, lasting 10 to 20 hours, are believed to be used in courtship and are performed as the whales migrate south from the Arctic and during winter breeding time in the tropics.

Although big animals often have deep voices, enormous humpbacks can sing far higher than even the shrillest human soprano. That may be because high sounds travel farther in the coastal shallows where humpbacks like to sing.

Male jumping spiders in Arizona perform courtship music by drumming with their front legs.

Spiders Feel the Beat

For male jumping spiders in the Sonoran Desert of Arizona, making themselves heard can be a life-and-death matter. Unlike web-spinning spiders, jumping spiders actively hunt their prey, and females even pounce on and devour males of their own kind.

To avoid that fate, male jumping spiders make music when they're looking for a mate. They drum a complicated little rhythm to tell females they want to breed. The song reaches the females through vibrations they feel with their feet. According to researchers, male spiders that drum on sand or stones may not be heard (or felt), and are more likely to miss out on mating—and to be eaten. Sensible spider musicians approach females on dried leaf litter. Dried leaves vibrate better so female spiders can feel the beat.

Bladder grasshoppers use a pitch that can be heard over other jungle sounds.

chapter 5

Ultrasound
Silent Music to Your Ears

SQUEAK

SQUEAK

Operatic mice? It's true—but the music is so shrill humans need special equipme to hear it.

All day long, the caged laboratory mice are kept busy. They run mazes. They press buttons. But when the researchers go home, the mice are left to themselves. If the mood is right, they strike up a song.

It's true. Mice sing. People have known for a long time that mice squeak and even that they call using sounds too shrill for us to hear. But only recently have researchers learned that mice are operatic stars in a world inaudible to people—the world of ultrasound.

Recorded on special equipment, male lab mice are shown to sing almost like songbirds. Individuals perform a variety of songs and phrases. Like Elvis, singers can be identified by their signature tunes. These elaborate mouse serenades last several minutes and are apparently meant to win the hearts of listening females.

Animal songs can make use of every imaginable sound—even if humans and some other creatures can't hear them. The discovery that animals can perform songs too shrill for our ears is a good example of how natural wonders go unnoticed when they are beyond human perception.

Many bats use ultrasonic sonar to "see" where they are going. Male greater sac-winged bats also use ultrasound to make music. These bats perform some of the most musically rich and complex songs outside the world of songbirds.

Greater sac-winged bats live in cave or tree-hole colonies throughout much of Central and South America. Males often sing short songs to warn other males away from their harem of females. Like many birds, neighboring males will sing back and forth in song "duels." To impress females, they will hover above their object of affection and serenade her with long, complex songs of whistles, trills, and bursts of noise. Each singer appears to have a distinctive song set—a repertoire—all his own.

Humans are unable to hear the high-pitched singing of China's concave-eared torrent frogs.

The concave-eared torrent frog was recently shown to be as talented as it is rare. Found in central China, the frog lives among rocks and plants near steep, wilderness streams. During the rainy breeding season, male frogs climb into streamside plants and sing. But the rain also means that trickling brooks become loud, rushing torrents.

Unlike other frogs, torrent frogs warble melodically the way birds do and even use ultrasound. Torrent frogs are the only amphibians known to do this, and researchers think the super-shrill singing may help the frogs make themselves heard above the thundering, low-frequency noise of water.

The ears of greater wax moths are specially designed to hear ultrasonic sounds.

Moths Play Ultrasonic Name That Tune

For female greater wax moths, music appreciation isn't just a hobby; it's a survival skill. Male greater wax moths make ultrasonic music by rubbing parts of their wings together. Females give a visual display of wing flicking to beckon Romeo closer. The problem is that moth music sounds similar to the ultrasonic *chirps* bats use to navigate in the dark. Females that mistake the two sounds and flick their wings for an approaching bat are likely to be eaten.

Timing is everything. Moth chirps are shorter and faster than the slightly longer bat sounds, and females can usually tell the difference. However, female moths prefer males that sing longer chirps. This means performing males have to try to seem irresistible without sounding too much like a hunting bat.

Blue-throated humming-birds cannot hear ultrasonic sounds even though they can sing in that range.

chapter 6

Predators
Songs in the Key of Yikes!

whiiine

chuck

Tasty tunes! Their singing makes túngara frogs easy to find for hungry fringe-lipped bats.

ity the poor túngara frog. Just when he happens upon the perfect song for winning female affection, he finds out that the biggest fan of his new tune is a frog-eating bat.

When the rains come to the forests of Central America, male túngara frogs sing in solitude or in large choruses to attract mates. Their song is a long *whine* (like the sound of a child imitating an airplane), often followed by an abrupt *chuck.* Scientists believe the *chuck* part of the song evolved only recently. Other related frogs only whine their music. Females really like the *chuck,* and males discovered that the sound attracted more mates.

The story might have a happy ending, if it weren't for fringe-lipped bats. After dark, these bats wing through the lowland forests of South and Central America listening for prey. Silent frogs are safe. Frogs singing the *whine* part of their song are also apparently difficult for bats to find. The túngara frog

chucks, however, give the game away: the bats zero in and eat the singer.

Interestingly, solitary túngara frogs sing only the *whine* part of their tune. With no other males to compete with, a lone singer can play it safe and still sound good to females. In a group of singers, male frogs have to put their best song forward. They add the *chucks,* taking their chances with the bats to increase their sex appeal.

nimal songs are intended to attract potential mates or to warn rival males. When predators are listening in, the challenge is all about getting a musical message across without getting eaten in the process. Even hunting humans sometimes rely on animal mating sounds. Bugling like an elk or grunting like a moose is an effective way to attract males anxious to defend their territory or protect their females.

It's smart to be shy. Male silver perch sto singing when hungry dolphir cruise by.

In the Atlantic inlets of North America, silver perch wait for dusk—that's show time. Males of this small fish species get together and form the fishy equivalent of an under-sea choir. Using muscles that vibrate their air bladder, they perform a chorus of soft, high-pitched knocks that can often be heard from shore.

Scientists believe the fish music is an important part of courtship. But the performances have an audience apart from listening females—dolphins. Bottlenose dolphins eat masses of silver perch. A chorus of male perch is like dinner music to dolphins.

The perch know this, and fall silent when dolphins are near. Research suggests that the fishy singers stop performing if they hear the high-pitched whistles dolphins use to communicate.

The skylark's song can tell a predator the performer is too fit to make an easy meal.

Skylarks Sing "You can't catch me"

In the clear morning air over an English field, a European skylark wings steeply upward, warbling his melody. Like many musical animals, the skylark sings to attract mates and defend his territory. But the song has another use—warning away hungry predators.

Skylarks are a favorite prey of merlins—a small, bird-catching falcon. When a merlin chases a skylark, the lark will often burst into song. The reason, say scientists, is to signal to the predator to give up the hunt. And it often works. Singing while flying, like singing while dancing, takes more energy. It appears to show that a bird is strong and unlikely to be easy prey.

Northern shrikes sing to attract mates. Sometimes their music also attracts other birds that become the shrike's lunch.

chapter 7

Duets

Connected by Music

HOOP, HOOP, HOOP

Siamang gibbon mates practice singing together until they are a perfect musical duo.

As the dawn mists drift skyward over an Indonesian rainforest, an eruption of whoops, screeches, and barks shatters the morning silence. The sounds seem to come from two places at once, braiding together into an eerie, beautiful music.

"Hoop, hoop, hoop," booms a deep voice in the canopy.

"Ooooeee yap yap yap," yodels the other.

The musicians are a pair of siamang gibbons, and their "opera" is the ape equivalent of a musical marriage vow. Siamangs are the largest and loudest of the gibbons. A sac on their throat inflates when they sing, working like a hollow chamber to resonate the sound and increase the volume. The ear-splitting sounds of siamangs can travel across rainforests. Duet bouts can last 15 minutes at a time.

Coordinated singing between two animals—usually a male and female—is called duetting. It's not common, and scientists still don't know why many animals do it. Duetting may let some animal pairs share the duty of defending a territory. It might also help mates keep track of one another. For listeners, duets may distinguish who has a mate from those still single and looking.

For siamangs, duets are also a sort of musical cement that helps strengthen their bond. When a siamang couple first pairs off, their songs are often out of sync. Coordinating the duet is crucial as they get to know each other, say scientists. Successful pairs go on to make beautiful music. Pairs that cannot mesh their music or that do not duet often may risk a breakup or, worse, losing their territory.

It takes two male long-tailed manakins years to synchronize their song-and-dance routine.

The duets of long-tailed manakins are unusual by duetting standards. For this bird, duetting partners aren't mates, they're males. Side by side on a high song perch, two singing bachelors perform a loud *toledo* song in unison. The show-biz duo includes a mentor bird and a younger apprentice. They perform and practice together for years until the youngster improves his skills at matching and synchronizing the song.

Female manakins listen for *toledo* duets that are seamlessly put together. The best duets get the most female visitors. When a female shows up, the two singers fly to a lower perch for a song-and-dance routine that ends with the older male mating with the female. Scientists say apprentices always leave this honor to their partner, since they too will one day sing and dance well enough to become a mentor. Sometimes, ten years will pass before that day arrives.

I'll meet you on the corner. Bushcrickets use duets for courtship and meeting up.

chirp

> click

Leafhopper pairs in southwestern Australia perform duets by sending vibrations along stalks of crabgrass.

Chirps to Stop Cheats

The scene is like a corny love opera. *"Chirp,"* sings the male bushcricket. *"Click,"* replies a female in the distance. With every singing response, the two insects draw closer until at last they embrace. Duets by Australian bushcrickets are performed by temporary male-female pairs. They are an agreement to mate—even before they meet. The call and response helps them to find each other.

Some crafty males keep quiet instead. These males eavesdrop on duetting pairs and try to intercept females. To stop these cheaters, duetting males have added an especially loud chirp to their song. Scientists believe they sing it over the female's song to prevent others from hearing and locating her.

Tuned for Change

Darwin's finches perform different tunes—smaller-beaked ones sing faster, higher songs.

Animal songs inspire human creativity with their beauty and wonder. But their purpose is to influence how animals behave, mate, and get along. Song can even play a part in the evolution of entirely new species.

Darwin's finches are a group of birds that lives on the Galápagos Islands. The finches are named after 19th-century naturalist Charles Darwin, who studied them before writing his famous theory about the origin of species. The various finch species—more than a dozen—have different beak sizes that reflect their different lifestyles. Large-beaked finches crunch seeds while smaller-beaked birds eat insects. One, the vampire finch, drinks the blood of living seabirds.

Singing is vital to many animals, and is also an important part of being human.

All are thought to have evolved from one ancestor species, and song likely played a key role. When the first finches arrived on the islands, slight natural variation in their beak sizes allowed them to eat a variety of foods.

Bigger- and smaller-beaked birds ate differently—and also sang differently. Beak size affects both the tone and speed at which a bird can sing.

Since females prefer the music of their own kind, larger-beaked, seed-eating females tended to mate with seed-eating males. And smaller-beaked, insect-eating females mated with insect-eating males. Over time, the finches evolved into many separate species.

The music of animals can help alter the course of evolution. When we open our ears to animal song, we begin to understand how amazing it is in other ways too—how many uses it has, how it can travel far, and how it's sometimes performed out of the range of human hearing. We also begin to understand how important song is to many creatures and how nature's often beautiful sounds help shape our wild world.

No one knows precisely when humans first made music, but the earliest musical instruments date back 40,000 years.

Further Reading

Beltz, Ellin. *Frogs: Inside Their Remarkable World*. Richmond Hill, ON: Firefly Books, 2005.

Chinery, Michael. *How Animals Communicate*. London: Anness Publishing, 2002.

Costanza, Stephen. *Mozart Finds a Melody*. New York: Henry Holt, 2004.

Doris, Ellen. *Ornithology (Real Kids/Real Science Books)*. New York: Thames & Hudson, 1994.

Elliott, Lang. *The Calls of Frogs and Toads*. Mechanicsburg, PA: Stackpole Books, 2004.

———. *Guide to Wildlife Sounds*. Mechanicsburg, PA: Stackpole Books, 2005.

Gallo, Frank, and Lori Lohstoeter. *Bird Calls*. San Francisco: Innovative Kids-Chronicle Books, 2001.

Green, Jen, Barbara Taylor, and John Farndon. *The Big Bug Book*. London: Lorenz Books, 2006.

Jenkins, Steve. *Slap, Squeak and Scatter: How Animals Communicate*. Boston: Houghton Mifflin, 2001.

Johnson, Jinny. *Simon & Schuster Children's Guide to Insects and Spiders*. New York: Simon & Schuster Children's Publishing, 1997.

Kalman, Bobbie. *How Animals Communicate*. St. Catherines, ON: Crabtree Publishing, 1996.

Latimer, Jonathan, Karen Stray Nolting, and Roger Tory Peterson. *Backyard Birds (Peterson Field Guides for Young Naturalists)*. Boston: Houghton Mifflin,1999.

McGrath, Susan. *How Animals Talk (Kids Want To Know)*. New York: Scholastic, 1999.

Niz, Xavier. *Animals Communicating*. Mankato, MN: Capstone Press, 2005.

Sayre, April Pulley. *Secrets of Sound: Studying the Calls and Songs of Whales, Elephants, and Birds (Scientists in the Field)*. Boston: Houghton Mifflin, 2002.

Schlein, Miriam, and Daniel Kirk. *Hello, Hello!* New York: Simon & Schuster, 2002.

Tatham, Betty. *How Animals Communicate*. New York: Scholastic Library, 2004.

Taylor, Barbara. *Apes and Monkeys*. London: Anness Publishing, 2004.

Wood, Audrey, and Robert Florczak. *Birdsong*. San Diego: Harcourt Children's Books, 1997.

Selected Bibliography

Andersson, M. 1994. *Sexual Selection*. Princeton, NJ: Princeton University Press.

Beecher, M.D., and S.E. Campbell. 2005. The role of unshared songs in singing interactions between neighbouring song sparrows. *Animal Behaviour* 70: 1297–304.

Behr, O., and O. von Helversen. 2004. Bat serenades—complex courtship songs of the sac-winged bat *(Saccopteryx bilineata)*. *Behavioral Ecology and Sociobiology* 56: 106–15.

Bostwick, K.S., and R.O. Prum. 2005. Courting birds sing with stridulating feathers. *Science* 309: 736.

Brantley, R.K., and A.H. Bass. 1994. Alternative male spawning tactics and acoustic signals in the plainfin midshipman fish *Porichthys notatus* Girard (Teleostei, Science Batrachoididae). *Ethology* 96: 213–32.

Catchpole, C.K., and P.J.B. Slater. 1995. *Bird Song: Biological Themes and Variations*. Cambridge, UK: Cambridge University Press.

Cresswell, W. 1994. Song as a pursuit-deterrent signal, and its occurrence relative to other anti-predation behaviours of skylark *(Alauda arvensis)* on attack by merlins *(Falco columbarius)*. *Behavioral Ecology and Sociobiology* 34: 217–34.

Elias, D.O, E.A. Hebets, R.R. Hoy, and A.C. Mason. 2004. Seismic signals are crucial for male mating success in a visual specialist jumping spider (Araneae: Salticidae). *Animal Behaviour* 69: 931–38.

Elliott, K. 2002. Singing fish. *Discovery* 31: 29–33.

Feng, A.S., P.M. Narins, Chun-He Xu, Wen-Yu Lin, Zu-Lin Yu, Qiang Qiu, Zhi-Min Xu, and Jun-Xian Shen. 2006. Ultrasonic communication in frogs. *Nature* 440: 333–36.

Galeotti, P., R. Sacchi, D. Pellitteri Rosa and M. Fasola. 2004. Female preference for fast-rate, high-pitched calls in Hermann's tortoise *Testudo hermanni*. *Behavioral Ecology* 16: 301–8.

Geissmann, T., and M. Orgeldinger. 2000. The relationship between duet songs and pair bonds in siamangs, *Hylobates syndactylus*. *Animal Behaviour* 60: 805–9.

Godard, R. 1991. Long-term memory of individual neighbours in a migratory songbird. *Nature* 350: 228–29.

Hammond, T.J., and W.J. Bailey. 2003. Eavesdropping and defensive auditory masking in an Australian bushcricket, Caedicia (Phaneropterinae: Tettigoniidae: Orthoptera). *Behaviour* 140: 79–95.

Holy, T.E., and G. Zhongsheng. 2005. Ultrasonic songs of male mice. *PLOS Biology* 3: 2177–86.

Jones, G., A. Barabas, W. Elliott, and S. Parsons. 2002. Female greater wax moths reduce sexual display behavior in relation to the potential risk of predation by echolocating bats. *Behavioral Ecology* 13: 375–80.

Lardner, B., and M. bin Lakim. 2002. Tree-hole frogs exploit resonance effects. *Nature* 420: 475.

Luczkovich, J.J., Daniel, H.J., III, Hutchinson, M., Jenkins, T., Johnson, S.E., Pullinger, R.C., and Sprague, M.W. 2000. Sounds of sex and death in the sea: bottlenose dolphin whistles suppress mating choruses of silver perch. *Bioacoustics* 10: 323–34.

Mennill, D.J., and L.M. Ratcliffe. 2004. Overlapping and matching in the song contests of black-capped chickadees. *Animal Behaviour* 67: 441–50.

Mercado, E., and L. Neil Frazer. 1999. Environmental constraints on sound transmission by humpback whales. *The Journal of the Acoustical Society of America* 106: 3004–16.

Myrberg, A.A., Jr., and R.J. Riggio. 1985. Acoustically mediated individual recognition by a coral reef fish *(Pomacentrus partitus)*. *Animal Behaviour* 33: 411–16.

Podos, J. 2001. Correlated evolution of morphology and vocal signal structure in Darwin's finches. *Nature* 409: 185–88.

Prestwich, K.N., and K. O'Sullivan. 2005. Simultaneous measurement of metabolic and acoustic power and the efficiency of sound production in two mole cricket species (Orthoptera: Gryllotalpidae). *Journal of Experimental Biology* 208: 1495–512.

Ryan, M. editor. 2005. *Anuran Communication.* Washington: Smithsonian Institution Press.

Saarikettu, M., J.O. Liimatainen, and A. Hoikkala. 2005. The role of male courtship song in species recognition in *Drosophila montana*. *Behavioural Genetics* 35: 257–63.

Sjare, B., I. Stirling, and C. Spencer. 2003. Structural variation in the songs of Atlantic walruses breeding in the Canadian High Arctic. *Aquatic Mammals* 29: 297–318.

Stewart, M.M. and P.J. Bishop. 1994. Effects of increased sound level of advertisement calls on calling male frogs, *Eleutherodactylus coqui*. *Journal of Herpetology* 28: 46–53.

Sueur, J. and T. Aubin. 2004. Acoustic signals in cicada courtship behaviour (order Hemiptera, genus *Tibicina*). *Journal of Zoology (London)* 262: 217–24.

Trainer, J.M., D.B. McDonald, and W.A. Learn. 2002. The development of coordinated singing in cooperatively displaying long-tailed manakins. *Behavioral Ecology* 13: 65–69.

Turner, J.S. 2002. *The Extended Organism: The Physiology of Animal-Built Structures.* Cambridge: Harvard University Press.

Von der Emde, G., J. Mogdans, and B.G. Kapoor, editors. 2003. *The Senses of Fish: Adaptations for the Reception of Natural Stimuli.* New York: Springer.

West, M.J., and A.P. King. 1990. Mozart's Starling. *American Scientist* 78: 106–14.

Index

Acknowledgments

I would like to thank Professor Daniel Mennill at the Department of Biological Sciences, University of Windsor, Ontario, for his review of the material in this book and for his comments and suggestions. I would also like to thank Elizabeth McLean, Li Eng-Lodge, and Antonia Banyard for their fine work putting this together. And, as always, thanks to Hannah, Laura, and Priscilla for their support and patience.

Photo credits